Paganism

An Introductory Guide

Pagan holidays, beliefs, gods and goddesses, symbols, rituals, practices, and much more!

By Riley Star

Foreword

For those who answer the spiritual call of paganism, an "image" problem is almost inevitable. All too commonly the simplistic definition of "pagan" is "not Christian," and with that comes a knee-jerk fear of devil worship and evil deeds. Nothing could be farther from the truth.

Strip the word "pagan" of such negative connotations, and forget that the Christian church created the label as a pejorative. Then, "pagan" simply denotes religions practiced before the spread of Christianity after the first century.

Unfortunately, most of those early forms of worship did and do run counter to accepted Christian practice and belief. That is where problems begin to arise.

Christianity claims to worship the "one true God," while pagans are polytheistic, venerating multiple gods from multiple traditions. In the pagan worldview, "deity" is present in all things, not embodied in a single form.

Clearly, the essential conflict with the dominant Christian belief in Europe and the Western world is unavoidable. Any faith that, by definition, worships one god has to see the worship of all others as heresy.

Traditionally, the Christian church has not been sufficiently tolerant to find common ground with pagans who worship Mother Earth or who recognize a universal intelligence inherent in all creation.

Practicing pagans have been branded (sometimes literally) as heretics and persecuted for our beliefs for hundreds of years.

In the 17th century, however, and roughly concurrent with the rise of the cultural and artistic movement known as Romanticism, a kind of pagan renaissance began to be seen.

This renewed interest in the old earth-centric religions led to the rise of modern neo-pagan faiths. The consequences of that spiritual rebirth are the real topic of this book.

It is important to understand that "paganism" is a catchall term that encompasses a number of philosophies. Any writer who tries to tackle "paganism" as a subject is forced to make choices about what to discuss in order to reasonably narrow the material.

The hope is that by highlighting aspects of exemplar pagan philosophies it will be possible to accurately express what it means to walk through the world with a pagan mindset. I will attempt to do that with three examples: Wicca, Druidry, and Odinism.

I chose Wicca because the general public is fairly familiar with its existence. Druidism comes from a similar branch of Celtic origin and so is a logical extension of the Wiccan discussion. Odinism, however, is more Germanic and Scandinavian in origin and will allow us to look at a different pantheon of gods.

Please understand from the beginning that these are only

three paths among many. I am a follower of Wicca, but I am not advocating that you walk the same path, nor am I recommending any direction for your personal journey.

Because many pagans are sole practitioners drawing from a number of traditions, it is, in my opinion, impossible to offer a definitive explanation of paganism in all its possible expressions.

In many ways, I wish we could just sit down and have a conversation because all pagan faiths are strongly experiential.

We all have a great deal to learn from one another and as we live and learn, we should make adjustments to our spiritual lives according to new understanding and insights.

You will never be the same kind of pagan I am. Although my path is Wiccan, I do not belong to a coven and I have a relationship with gods and goddesses from other traditions in addition to the Lady and the Lord.

Unlike organized Christian religion, paganism does not burden its followers with needless dogma. The point is to find and to follow your own spiritual path wherever it may lead you.

If you are coming from a Christian background, your natural inclination may be to look for a book or "rules" or "laws" as you begin this new journey. Although you may find many learned texts that will enhance the depth of your understanding, there is no pagan "Bible."

My goal is to help you to understand that although highly ethical in its principles, paganism places the responsibility for right action squarely on the shoulders of the practitioner.

The emphasis on self-responsibility is so strong that in some respects, you may find pagan systems to be more rigidly ethical than their Christian counterparts.

By the end of the text, I hope to have dispelled some of the more common myths about paganism and to have offered some assistance to those of my readers who are taking their first steps down a new spiritual course.

This is not intended to be a textbook or even a set of instructions, but rather shared information and observations from a fellow seeker.

Also, to be a practicing pagan, you do not have to engage in elaborate rituals with groups of people. You can incorporate aspects of your spiritual quietly and simply into your everyday life.

"Mindfulness" is a powerful spiritual act. Stopping to appreciate a bird song or to watch the sunrise or set is, for a pagan, an act of worship. Beginning and ending your day with a few words of gratitude to the deities you follow will bring you into closer relationship with them.

Pagans, like any other religious people, can be guilty of just showing up for major holidays, but in my opinion, spirituality that is lived daily is much richer and more rewarding. That is my way, but it does not have to be yours.

In the end, the best advice I can offer is to open your heart and listen. The gods and goddesses with whom you are meant to work will find you. Never resist the call of your own heart and mind as you find your way in the world.

Table of Contents

Table of Contents

Table of Contents

Chapter 1 - Paganism as a Concept

Critics of those who choose to follow ancient spiritual traditions use the term "paganism" as if it refers to a single religion or body of belief.

Such usage is inaccurate, especially when the word "pagan" is employed as a means to contrast every other philosophy as "wrong" when held up against the one "true" path.

Of course, that path in the Western world is the Christian faith, which I in no way mean to disparage or to denigrate. To pagans, no path is more valid than any other.

My way may not be right for you, or yours for me, but if we are ethical pagans, we respect each other's spiritual position without judgment.

And we must extend this tolerance even to those who criticize and condemn us – including Christians.

Clearly to be pagan is to be "not Christian," but that does not mean that pagans worship the devil, the dark side, or any other characterization of the force of entropy and negativity in the world.

Behaving badly toward Christians, however, will do nothing to dispel their negative mindset or to validate our own ethical position. In all things we get back in equal measure that which we give, therefore tolerance even in the face of censure is essential.

If you are a Christian reading this material, it's important for you to understand that pagans do not see the world as locked in a struggle between the forces of good and evil. It is simplistic and inaccurate to assume that if a person does not worship the Christian God, they must therefore worship the Christian Satan.

Since pagans do not recognize the Christian belief system, such an either / or scenario is not possible within the confines of our faith.

Pagans of all sorts are highly ecumenical in their approach to being in relationship with Mother Earth and, in fact, with the Universe itself.

Deity is immanent in all things, including each of us. All paths – including Christianity – are valid and demand out respect. The greatest spiritual exercise lies in finding the way that is right for you. Never allow that choice to be dictated to you and never attempt to dictate it to anyone else.

What is Paganism?

Offering a comprehensive definition of paganism is not as simple then as it might appear on first blush.

Given the constraints of language it is impossible to explain paganism without referring to the advent of Christianity. Without the rise of the Christian religion, no other faith would be referred to as "pagan."

Understandably to many pagans, that fact alone is offensive, but given how the words are used in our language, it is fair to say than any religion that is not Christian is pagan. (Presuming you approach the subject from the dominant Western perspective of Christianity.)

In order to blunt that potentially offensive definition, the best we can do is settle on the fact that a pagan, or more accurately, a neo-pagan, is someone who is inspired by the old religions that existed before Christianity.

It's best to regard the distinction as chronological rather than qualitative.

Further Clarification of Terms

Also, to further clarify terms, I will use "pagan" and "neo-pagan" interchangeably. There are those purists who would prefer the word "pagan" to be used only in reference to the old religions, and "neo-pagan" to refer to the renaissance in pagan spirituality evident from the 17th century forward, but for the purposes of this text, I find that distinction overly confusing.

We must also consider the matter of capitalization. Many pagans feel that the word should be capitalized to accord their spirituality equal respect with other religions like Christianity that are consistently capitalized in written texts. Personally, I find this to be a trivial matter, and will, again use both forms interchangeably.

Finally, it's important to consider the use of the word "religion" itself. To distinguish paganism from other faiths, it must be emphasized that pagans recognize the ascendancy and divinity of nature.

We are discussing a strongly earth-based spirituality. Pagans often have a problem with references to their belief structure as a "religion." The world implies a degree of organization, structure, and dogma that simply isn't present in the pagan world.

For this reason, many practicing pagans prefer to have their path described as a "philosophy" or a "way of life" rather than as a "religion."

At best, "pagan" is an umbrella term that refers to any one of a number of belief systems that reach back beyond Christianity to an older way. My use of the term "religion" in referenced to paganism is purely utilitarian.

I do not mean to suggest that any of the spiritual paths we will discuss is chiseled in stone. Again, all pagan faiths accommodate the sanctity of the individual journey as it is shaped by a person's life experiences.

In fact, language is one of the greatest challenges in discussing paganism. For instance, it would be fair to say that witches are pagans, but not all pagans are witches.

These distinctions rapidly deteriorate into a slippery slope of misunderstanding and obfuscation.

Some General Statements About Paganism

The pagan worldview has been described as one that relies on a belief in magic, which is a common if fuzzy understanding for the layperson.

This is true, in part, because paganism has proven to be an excellent source of plot material for epic fantasy fiction. This fact does not, however, negate the accuracy of associating magic with pagan spirituality.

Most pagans do believe in the practice of "magic" as a further means to refine their understanding of and relationship with nature.

Using this as an example, some general statements can be made that are valid for most pagan belief systems.

- Pagan beliefs extend to the time of the deities that were revered before the rise of Christianity.

- Paganism is polytheistic, worshipping many gods and goddesses rather than one.

- Pagans believe in the existence of a number of magical creatures.

- Pagans believe in the presence of spirits in our lives with whom we may communicate, which is in keeping with veneration of the ancestors.

- Paganism is pantheistic, regarding all of nature as inherently sacred. The landscape itself is considered to be divine.

- Paganism is animistic, holding that all beings and even inanimate objects have souls and are connected by spiritual and universal energy

Pagan communities celebrate rites of passage in life including, but not limited to baby blessings, marriages (more commonly called handfastings) and funerals. Groups also have initiatory rites.

With some variation in the names of the associated events, the pagan calendar follows the Wheel of the Year, which includes:

- Samhain
- Winter Solstice
- Imbolc
- Spring Equinox
- Beltaine

- Summer Solstice
- Lughnasadh
- Autumn Equinox

It is common for pagans to have some form of ritual dress, often long robes, and to use ritual adornments and tools with symbolic significance.

These may include knives, staffs, and wands among others. Many pagans have body modifications like tattoos and piercings that are also an expression of their spirituality.

Paganism is not, however, a one-size-fits-all endeavor. Many pagans live as solitary practitioners in harmonious relationship with gods and goddesses of multiple traditions with whom they feel a close affinity.

These spiritual seekers find comfort and guidance in rituals, symbols, and objects of their own making and design.

4 Myths About Paganism

- **Pagans want to amass material wealth**. – False. Pagans regard the emphasis on consumerism in the modern world to be evidence of spiritual poverty.

- **Pagans engage in sexual debauchery**. – False. The Pagan moral code is often stricter than that practiced in secular society.

- **Pagans worship Satan**. – False. The deities worshipped by pagans predate Christianity and the

Christian Satan by thousands of years.

- **Pagans practice black magic**. – False. Pagans do not believe in the use of magic for ill intent, nor are they in favor of animal sacrifice.

12 Truths about Paganism

- Pagans teach that knowledge and wisdom is an inherent part of all humans and must simply be accessed by lowering our barriers through spiritual practice including meditation.

- Pagans are pantheistic, regarding the entire universe as a manifestation of deity.

- Pagans are polytheistic, worshiping more than one god.

- Pagans venerate and work to conserve nature.

- Pagans are inclusive of both the male and female spirit.

- Pagans emphasize individual and social responsibility.

- Pagans are community (clan / tribe) minded.

- Pagans are accepting of private, sole spiritual practice.

- Pagans emphasize harmony and balance.

- Pagans believe that no quality when displayed in excess is a positive.

- Pagans are tolerant and do not judge.

- Pagans have no concept of sin, but they do recognize wrong that arises from bad choices and poor actions.

Neo-Pagan Movements

The breadth of the Neo-Pagan revival is so great that only an author willing (and sufficiently knowledgeable) to undertake an encyclopedic work could ever hope to include them all. I'm not that author!

My purpose here is only to show you that there is a

different way of seeing the world and of walking the earth spiritually. It is your task to find the specific path that resonates with your soul.

For our purposes, I will be looking at three paths: Wicca, Druidry, and Odinism. There are many paths you may choose to follow, and many sects and interpretations within those paths. The following sections are only partial lists. To be a pagan is, by definition, also to be a student.

Wicca

- British Traditional Wicca
- Gardnerian Wicca
- Alexandrian Wicca
- Algard Wicca
- Blue Star Wicca
- Celtic Wicca
- Sacon Wicca
- Dianic Wicca
- Faery Wicca
- New Reformed Orthodox order of the Golden Dawn
- Rowan Tree Church
- Stregheria

Germanic Traditions

- American Asatru
- Ring of Troth
- Odinism
- International Asatru-Odinic Alliance
- Theodism

- Íslenska Ásatrúarfélagið
- Foreningen Forn Sed
- Samfälligheten för Nordisk Sed
- Swedish Asatru Assembly
- Åsatrufellesskapet Bifrost
- Odin Brotherhood
- Wotanism

Celtic

- Celtic Reconstructionism
- Reformed Druids of North America
- Order of Bards, Ovates, and Druids
- Monastic Order of Avallon
- Ár nDraíocht Féin

Chapter 2 - The Wiccan Way

Wicca is probably the best known of the neo-pagan faiths. It is best described as an experiential way of being in the world. Its guiding principle is the Wiccan Rede, "And ye harm none, do what ye will."

As a living religion, Wicca is in a constant state of evolution that allows for sole practitioners to draw from the well of their own life experience and to develop individual rituals and observances.

Wicca derives primarily from rites grounded in ancient Druidic and shamanistic Western European traditions. There is no central, governing Wiccan "church" or specific "holy" book with codified behavioral instructions or admonitions. Many Wiccans do keep a "book of shadows" as a personal record of specific spells and rituals, but this is more akin to keeping a journal.

Wiccans who belong to a coven formally declare their intent
to follow Wicca and then undergo an initiation witnessed
by the group. In coven life, they become a part of a
community of belief, and practice their faith in the
company of like-minded individuals.

Solitary practitioners, on the other hand, pledge themselves
to Wicca after arriving at the decision through private
introspection and study. The form that their personal
dedication assumes is as individualistic as the means of
their ritualistic observance of Wiccan holidays and rites.

Both roads to Wicca are regarded as equally valid, which in
itself illustrates the tolerant nature of the faith.

Because the Wiccan belief structure, regardless of form, is
remarkably free of dogma, the religion focuses on the here
and now.

Wiccans believe that Deity infuses all of nature so that the
flowering meadow, the majestic desert, and the shady
forest are all natural, sanctified cathedrals where the Earth
constantly speaks to us.

The greater our awareness of our place on the active wheel
of life, the more we are able to hear those messages and to
act upon them. This is why many Wiccan rites are
performed outdoors and occasionally in the nude (skyclad).

Major Life Experiences

Wiccans celebrate all the major life experiences including birth, love, sex, and death. The belief in reincarnation is prevalent among Wiccans, but there is no concept of going to heaven as a reward for good and moral behavior in the present life. By the same token, there is also no notion of hell as a place of punishment.

Death is simply another stage of life to be revered and experienced. Wiccans recognize the physical world as being comprised of multiple layers of reality each varying in weight and intensity. No single variation is seen as the ultimate or purest expression of what it means to be alive, but each teaches unique lessons in living.

The individual Wiccan looks to his own senses as a guide to what is true and functional in the context of his beliefs and adjusts those beliefs accordingly.

Once an experience has been lived, it is then "owned" and becomes a part of who you are. Reading, studying, and debating can never take the place of a first-person experience.

Emphasis on a Connection with Nature

The Wiccan calendar observes the cycle of the seasons through a series of eight major holidays or "sabbats." (As you will see from the previous list in Chapter 1, these are the major observances of the basic pagan calendar with slightly different names.)

- **Samhain** (October 31) is a day set aside to pay tribute to the ancestors who have gone on before. Samhain is regarded as a time when the border between this world and other realms is lifted. You may also see this sabbat referred to as Halloween, Last Harvest, Ancestor Night, or the Feast of the Dead.

- **Midwinter** (observed around December 23) is a day that symbolizes the rebirth of the god. It may also be called Yule or Winter Rite and corresponds with the Winter Solstice, which is the shortest day of the year.

- **Candelmas** (February 1) is a celebration of the renewal of nature and the coming of spring. It is an observance during which Wiccans look at the past year and its achievements and set goals or make resolutions for the coming year. This sabbat may also be called Imbolc, Oimelc, Brigit, or Brigid.

- **Ostara** (around March 21) is timed with the Spring Equinox when the length of day and night is equal. As a symbol of fertility and rebirth, the egg is strongly evident in the celebration of this sabbat, which includes egg rolling and egg fights. Wiccans often put out milk and food for dwarves and fairies during Osara, and it's common to attempt to reach the ancestors during this time by gazing into bowls of clear spring water.

- **Beltaine** (May 1) denotes a high period of natural fertility and is a merging of traditions from both

Gaelic and Germanic belief. It is a day of love and is often the time at which engagements are arranged and marriages solemnized.

- **Midsummer** (June 21) corresponds with the Summer Solstice, which is the longest day of the year and the shortest night. It is at this point of the cycle that the wheel begins to turn toward the coming dark of winter. Midsummer may also be referred to as Mother Night, Litha, and Samradh.

- **August Eve** (August 1 or 2) is a time of thanks to the earth for the bounty of the harvest. It is another day when marriages are often performed and is also a popular time for coven initiations to take place. This sabbat is also called Lughnasadh, Lammas, the Bread Harvest, or the First Harvest.

- **Harvest Home** (September 21) corresponds with the Autumnal Equinox and marks the beginning of fall. Friends and family quietly and peacefully observe a ritual of Thanksgiving at this time. Harvest Home may also be referred to as Second Harvest, Mabon, or Foghar.

Wiccan rituals are often held outdoors as a means of tapping into the deeper connection with the Earth. The goal is to walk lightly on Mother Earth and to learn from her teachings.

It is common for Wiccans to dedicate themselves to environmental causes and to live as vegetarians or vegans.

An Awareness of Magic

Some Wiccans recognize and use magic, whether that be a minor spell to help locate a lost item or an elaborate ritual designed to focus power and to commune directly with deity.

Magic is another tool to help the individual to get in touch with their life's purpose and to become more directly aligned with their higher self.

It is inaccurate, however, to equate the words "Wicca" and "witch" as interchangeable although you will commonly see the term "witchcraft" used to describe Wiccan rituals and spells.

Simply put, you can be a Wiccan who does not practice magic or a witch who does not follow Wicca. Both a Wiccan and a witch, however, would be termed a pagan since both are followers of one of the many earth-based religions.

Wicca is NOT Devil Worship

Wiccans do not believe in Satan. They do not recognize a conflict in the world between a force of supreme good and one of supreme evil.

The Christian church, in waging a war against Satanism, posits that a pact has been made with the devil by followers who engage in practices of black magic including animal and human sacrifice.

Wiccans have absolutely no part of such beliefs or activities.

It is especially important to understand that in terms of moral oversight, pagan communities are not licentious dens of child abusers and serial adulterers.

If anything, the code of conduct is as strict or stricter in a Wiccan coven than in many Christian settings, even in the face of an open attitude toward sexuality.

In the Wiccan world, covens typically do not accept students until they are 21 years of age or older, reasoning, rightly, that it would be unacceptable and inappropriate to expose younger individuals to rituals that include sexual symbolism and even nudity.

(Ritual nudity, referred to as "working skyclad," is always an optional practice.)

Although it may be difficult for fearful detractors to understand, Wicca is based on a philosophy of personal responsibility that emphasizes the edict to do no harm. It is a principled and ethical belief structure.

Wiccans do not solicit members. We do not allow children into ritual observances. There is no requirement for nudity or sexual activity.

If any group calling itself "Wiccan" asks prospective members to do any of these things – or in fact anything that feels uncomfortable or "wrong" – you are not working with a true Wiccan community.

Always follow your "gut." It is one of the strongest voices Nature has given you. If something does not feel right, leave. If you suspect children or young people are being harmed or mistreated in any way, contact the authorities. This is precisely the kind of right action that real Wiccan belief demands of us.

Wiccan Principles and Beliefs

Because Wiccans accept that there is more than one path to "God" (or gods), members do not proselytize (recruit). Each individual must find his or her own spiritual path. Those who are meant to be Wiccans will find Wicca. It's just that simple.

It follows naturally then, that since Wiccans do not see the world in terms of a cosmic struggle between ultimate good and evil, there is no need for exclusivity.

Followers of Wicca are free to practice other religious observances and to recognize and to worship more than one deity.

Overall, Wiccans follow seven major beliefs whose expression and observances varies by coven and individual. Each one is discussed below.

1. Deity in Polarity

While the single divine force that gives universal life is called spirit or deity, it has no confining definition ordered by time, space, or gender.

Deity does, however, have separate aspects, including male and female as depicted in the God and Goddess.

The equality of the God and Goddess is a sacred dynamic central to the practice of Wicca. The two aspects are separate but inseparable halves of the same whole, existing in polarity.

Both are warm and loving, approachable and reachable. The God and Goddess are omnipresent and cannot exist independently one from the other.

2. An Immanent Deity

Deity as a sacred life force is inherent in all people and in all things. Each of us is part of the divine as are all things around us. This sacred way of thinking gives Wiccans an instinctive respect for all beings and for the natural world in which they live.

The concept of immanent deity is not so much the idea that a blade of grass or a random bit of stone possesses a soul of its own, but rather that we are all part of a greater universal "soul."

3. Earth and Its Divinity

Given this belief, it should be easy to see the earth as the greatest of all the tangible manifestations of deity, and one that is closely tied to that aspect of the deity we call the Goddess. The earth is the universal mother, giving birth to all things and then receiving them again in death.

Wicca emphasizes the earth's natural flow of power as expressed in the cycle of the seasons. Becoming attuned to earth energy and working with it is a special focus of the path and is at the heart of the Wiccan belief that there is a special imperative to responsibly care for Mother Earth as a sacred space.

Responsible actions in this regard might include following a vegetarian or a vegan diet and engaging in conservation projections and other aspects of environmental activism.

4. Sharpening Native Psychic Powers

According to Wiccan belief, we are each born with psychic abilities that can be sharpened to allow for better connection with the divine force.

With these abilities, a person can gain more information about the world at large than the five senses would normally allow and thus can perform acts well beyond the normal limitations of human action.

Meditation, ritual divination, and other forms of magical practice are all part of the Wiccan spiritual life and are called upon as a means of enhancing natural intuition to allow you to reach both inside and out with your psychic powers.

5. Belief in Magic

Magic is used by Wiccans to help negotiate the twists and turns of their spiritual journeys. The core purpose of the belief in magic is to facilitate transcendence of the ordinary as a tool of empowerment and growth.

Although many people find it an uncomfortable admission, most religions, including Christianity, do employ magical thinking; they simply use other names for what they are doing.

Perhaps the most striking example is that of the Christian

act of mass or communion in which the bread and wine of the sacrament are transformed into the body and blood of Jesus Christ.

The act of prayer is a way to communicate with the deity and to extend concentrated energy toward a desired outcome. Not all prayers (or spells) are designed to manifest an item or to set in motion a series of events.

Some simply ask for peaceful and wise acceptance of current circumstances and ask for the insight to act in a proper manner.

It is only semantics for one religion to call prayer an act of faith and another to describe it as a magical meditation. In Wicca, magic is never used as a means to make the natural world conform to the will of the practitioner.

6. Reincarnation

While the majority of Wiccans believe in reincarnation, there is debate over how the process works. The idea that human souls leave one body at death and enter another in a kind of rebirth is reasonably universal but whether this is a recycling of the same person's essence or a direct transfer is more difficult to sort out.

There is also widespread belief in the concept of a universal soul that is one within us all simultaneously. The universal soul experiences different realities and infinite possibilities. By branching out into different vessels it explores various lives that go toward creating a single experience of growth and understanding.

Each Wiccan must arrive at a personal understanding of reincarnation through meditation and self-awareness. As with all principles, the religion is highly accommodating of individual understanding.

7. Sex as a Sacred Act

In a faith where deity is revered in its male and female aspects, it should come as no surprise that the sexual union of consenting adults is seen as a sacred expression of those dual aspects. There is, however, no taboo or prejudice against homosexual unions.

The sexual act is also an expression of the fertile gifts of mother earth. Wicca is replete with sexual symbolism, which is why covens typically restrict membership to individuals age 21 or older.

The Threefold Law and the Wiccan Rede

Even though individual Wiccans must find their own ethical way in the world, the Wiccan Rede is taken as a guiding principle. "An it harm none, do as ye will."

The Rede can be likened to a sort of "Golden Rule" admonishing each of us to think before we act and speak and to refrain from taking actions or expressing thoughts and ideas that would be harmful to ourselves or to others.

The Rede issues a kind of challenge to act in accordance

with the highest purpose of the human will and in so doing, to infuse all aspects of our lives with spiritual awareness. All actions taken, decisions made, and ideas expressed should be in perfect accord and harmony with deity.

The Rede's emphasis on self-knowledge, empowerment, and personal responsibility is the highest expression of Wicca's ethical underpinnings.

Unlike Christianity, which places men's souls ever at risk of being tempted by the forces of evil, Wicca believes that each of us is a free soul with full control over the direction and purpose of our lives. In other words, the buck stops here.

There is no blaming Satan or the devil for an act that violates moral principle. Wicca doesn't let you get off that easy!

Many Wiccans find themselves drawn to the path for this very reason. We are not at the mercy of fate, but are rather engaged in the act of shaping the course of our lives every second and are completely responsible for every action -- good and bad.

The Rede is an important part of the process of integrating past experiences to positively influence future action, as is The Threefold Law.

This principle states that whatever you put into the world will come back to you three times. Positive energy begets positive energy and a smoother flow of life.

Together the Rede and the Threefold Law are touchstones illustrating that the choice to follow the Wiccan path is a personal dedication to live in the world in an ethical way.

As one of many earth-based religions, Wicca is one of the more popular of the pagan faiths and one that is especially accommodating of the experience of the individual practitioner.

Chapter 3 - Druidism

Wicca draws many principles from Neo-Druidism, which is also an earth religion promoting worship in harmony with nature. Druidism saw resurgence in Great Britain in the 17th and 18th century in tandem with the Romantic Movement and its glorification of Celtic culture. Significantly, many of the roots of modern Wicca were also established in the same period.

Within the following 100 years, the cultural emphasis of the new Druidic thought morphed into the spiritual movement we know today. Like Wiccans, Druids are staunch environmentalists and also believe in the veneration of the ancestors.

Thanks primarily to the figure of Merlin in the Arthurian legends, there is a popular perception of a "Druid" as a wise old wizard with a flowing white beard who goes around in robes advising kings and magically altering the course of events.

(Video games have done their fare share to promulgate this image as well.)

This stereotypical construct, while perhaps not entirely erroneous, is as limiting as the perception of a witch as a crone dressed in black wearing a pointed hat and riding a broom.

Neo-Druidism

As is the case with Wicca, Neo-Druidic beliefs are not tied to a specific systematic dogma. The basic organizational unit in most groups is the "grove." There are a number of Druidic governing bodies that oversee branches of the body of belief including:

- **The Ancient Order of Druids in America**, founded in 1912, a group that actually makes no claim to being descended from the ancient Druids, themselves. Instead the AODA traces its evolution from the "Druid Revival," which began 300 years ago.

  Styling itself as an "esoteric" society. There is an initiatory rite and three degrees: Druid Apprentice, Druid Companion, and Druid Adept conferred after a program of study that emphasizes the spiritual development of the individual. The Grand Grove oversees the Order, member Groves, and study groups.

See: aoda.org

- **The Reformed Druids of North America**, founded in 1963, at Carleton College in Northfield, Minnesota was originally nothing more than a tongue-in-cheek protest of the school's requirement that students attend religious services.

  Over the past 40 years, however, the group has grown into a spiritual movement focused on nature. Reformed Druids follow the festival days of the pagan tradition.

  Their gatherings include singing, chanting, prayers, and the ritual consumption of the Waters of Life (Scotch whisky and water.)

  See: rdna.info

- **The Order of Bards, Ovates, and Druids**, founded in 1964, divides membership into three working grades: Bards (artists, musicians, and songwriters), Ovates (healers, counselors, and helpers), and Druids (teachers and negotiators).

  Individual members and groups are free to choose their own pantheon of gods for worship, but most venerate the traditional gods and goddesses of the Celtic tradition (England, Scotland, Wales, and

Ireland). Many members of the Order prefer to function as solitary practitioners.

See: druidry.org

Druidry expresses the same connection to Mother Earth as other pagan traditions as well as strong ties to the ancestors. For Druids, nature is the highest expression of divinity and deity and thus is the central focus of the philosophy's veneration.

History of Neo-Druidry

Neo-Druidism draws heavily from the Celtic tradition, but because the ancient Celts did not leave a written record, there is considerable debate about what these people actually believed.

References to historical Druids first appear in the writings of the Romans, who described them as the fierce and bloodthirsty priests of the Celtic tribes. The Romans saw the Druids as a threat, massacring many of these warrior priests until the order died out.

Like many pagan faiths, Druidism enjoyed a renaissance during the Romantic movement of the 17th century, appearing first in Great Britain and then spreading around the world.

Early medieval writers held to the barbaric Roman characterization of the Druids, associating them with human sacrifice and pitting them against early Christians. By the late medieval period, however, a gradual reinvention began that ended with the druids being portrayed as national heroes not just in England, Scotland, and Ireland, but also in France and Germany.

These depictions were the first to suggest druids were elderly men with long white beards and robes.

An Anglican vicar, William Stukeley (1687-1765), self-identified as druid and wrote widely on the topic, claiming that sites like Stonehenge and Avebury were druid temples.

Stukeley believed that the druids practiced a monotheistic faith that was extremely similar to Christianity. His ideas touched off the formation of druidic societies, including the Ancient Order of Druids in 1781 that was heavily influenced by Freemasonry.

None of these groups could be described as religious in nature until a Welshman, Edward Williams, who later took the name Iolo Morganwg, claimed to be the last initiate of a druidic group with roots tracing back to the Iron Age.

A staunch Welch nationalist, he opposed the British monarchy and formed a religious group that he claimed worshipped a monotheistic deity in the ancient druidic tradition.

Others followed his example, resurrecting a kind of nationalistic role for the symbol of a wise, nature-worshipping priesthood as an enduring element of British history.

Even with the scant nature of the ancient writings -- and the archaeological revelation that Stonehenge had no druidic connection -- some "standards" of Druidic tradition became accepted as common knowledge, including:

- veneration of specific trees and plants (especially oaks and mistletoe)
- a role as tribal priests and philosophers
- skilled work in herbology, medicine, and astronomy
- service as politicians and diplomats

The modern Druid is not simply a robed re-enactor of his ancient forebearers' ritual practices, showing up at Stonehenge at dawn to celebrate the equinox, however. Instead, neo-Druids seek to bring ancient techniques of understanding and insight back into modern life to create greater balance between opposing but complementary forces (male and female, the sun and the moon) as well as among the elements of earth, fire, air, and water.

Modern Druidry attracts a mixed bag of adherents from all walks of life and all spiritual traditions. Its followers not only feel the pull of ancient places, but in the modern, technological world, the neo-Druid is also searching for his connection to the earth.

Some do, indeed, dress up in robes and celebrate rites at ancient sites, while others plant trees or work in small groups on conservation projects.

All feel a need to connect to the land and not just to be in nature, but also to be a part of nature. Like Wiccans, they celebrate the festivals that mark the pagan Wheel of the Year.

Druidism is even more strongly animistic than Wicca, holding that all of nature is imbued with spirit or soul. Some, in the Celtic tradition, believe that plants and animals are members of distinct tribes.

By working for environmental causes and seeking to halt rampant land development and unchecked pollution, Druids protect their brothers and sisters in the plant and animal worlds.

Druid Theology

Theologically, Druidry is a diverse philosophy, proving itself to be equally accommodating of both a monotheistic and a polytheistic tradition. When the Druid Revival began in the 17th and 18th centuries, Great Britain was a predominantly Christian nation. There was no burgeoning pagan movement until the early 20th century.

That movement did, however, create greater freedom for practicing Druids to move more strongly toward the Celtic gods and goddesses associated with their historical antecedents. In truth, Neopagan Druidry is much more directly tied to Goddess worship, although some groups opt for the middle-of-the-road reference to "Spirit" over a gender-specific deity.

Ancestor veneration and the preservation of national and tribal heritage is also central to the Druid belief structure with particular emphasis on the Iron Age Celts of Western Europe. Other groups within the great body of Druidry, however, find themselves more naturally attuned to Anglo-Saxon or Norse history and mythology.

There is a widespread, but not necessarily universal, acceptance of the principle of reincarnation and the idea that a soul can return to live another life in the body of either a human or of an animal.

Druid Ceremonies

Druid ceremonies typically are held in a circle around an altar or fire during the daylight hours. Assemblages at ancient sites like stone circles are common.

Both Stonehenge and Glastonbury are regarded as sacred spots (even though they have no valid connection to the early druids.) These spots attract Neo-Druid groups at major times of the year like the summer solstice.

Where robes are worn, color variations may signify grade within the order. For instance in the Order of Bards, Ovates, and Druids the respective color for each grade are blue, green, and white. Ritual staffs may also be carried,.

By the same token, however, many modern Druids do not wear any sort of ceremonial garb whatsoever and keep their philosophy private and highly personal.

The founder of the Order of Bards, Ovates, and Druids, Ross Nichols, borrowed the pagan calendar or Wheel of the Year from his friend Gerald Gardner, the founder of the line of Gardnerian Witches, a major branch of the Wiccan faith. Like their Wiccan brethren, Druids celebrate the equinoxes, solstices, and "cross quarter" days.

Other events, like Eisteddfod, are dedicated to the recitation of poetry and the performance of music by Bards. Such gatherings may be actual festivals or simple get-togethers at the local pub.

Common instruments include the guitar, flute, whistle, bagpipes, Celtic harp, and the bodhran, which is a traditional Celtic frame drum.

In Summary

In summary, the spiritual life of a Druid is one that is strongly in tune with nature and grounded in a sense of ancient connection. It can be a highly solitary path that draws the follower to high and lonely places where spirit dwells.

The Druid's Prayer, written by Iolo Morganwg, is used by many Druids and helps to convey a sense of what the philosophy is intended to cultivate in its followers:

> Grant, O Great Spirit/Goddess/God/Holy Ones, Thy Protection;
>
> And in protection, strength;
> And in strength, understanding;
> And in understanding, knowledge;
> And in knowledge, the knowledge of justice;
> And in the knowledge of justice, the love of it;
> And in that love, the love of all existences;
> And in the love of all existences, the love of Great Spirit/Goddess/God/Holy Ones/the Earth our mother, and all goodness.

Chapter 4 - Odinism

Unlike Wicca and Druidism, Odinism derives from Scandinavian and Germanic roots. In some traditions the term "Odinism" is held to be synonymous with Ásatrú, Wotanism, and Wodenism. There are, however, distinct differences.

Both Odinism and Ásatrú honor the pre-Christian Scandinavian pantheon, which includes Odin, Thor, Freyr, Freyja, and Heimdall among other deities.

Ásatrú, however, which was developed in the United States in the 1970s, is more focused on reconstructing the old religion to the point of dressing as Vikings and learning the old languages.

Odinists are more modern in their outlook, preferring to draw wisdom from the old ways, but seeking to bring those philosophical concepts into modern times.

Odinism is also more codified and defined than Ásatrú, encompassing a well-organized worldview, whereas Ásatrú is something of a "catchall" belief.

Wotanism was founded in the early 1990s and has strong associations with Aryan white supremacy movement. It is a neo-völkisch and ethnocentric philosophy.

The Wotanists do not just revere the Nordic or Scandinavian pantheon, but all the deities of Western European mythology.

Wodenism styles itself as a "reconstructed religion, spiritual path, mindset, kinship, appreciation, interest, relationship, and love, of the Wodenic pantheon." (See wodenism.com.)

Woden was the most widely known of the Anglo-Saxon gods whose name survives into modern times in the place names of many sites in England.

The UK-based Odinist Fellowship (see odinistfellowship.co.uk) declares outright that "Odinism is the original, indigenous faith of the English people" and goes on to describe it as the "heathen religion" practiced by the Angles, Saxons, Jutes and "related Teutonic peoples of the Continent."

The Odinist Pantheon

Odinists revere the High Gods of Asgarth, also known as the Æsir and Vanir. The deities have the ability to intervene in human lives and to change the course of nature.

The gods are not interested in having abased followers, so there is no bowing or kneeling in the Odinist belief structure. The gods are regarded as powerful allies and friends to be faced directly and proudly.

The pantheon includes:

- Odin, who values wisdom above all else.
- Thor, the hot-tempered and fierce god of thunder.
- Tyr, the god of war.

- Baldr, the son of Odin and his heir.
- Freyja, the goddess of love, fertility, sex, and war.
- Vidar, the god of silence and revenge.
- Bragi, the god of poetry.
- Heimdall, the guardian and god of light.
- Frigg, the goddess of marriage, motherhood, and the household.
- Njord, the god of seamanship and sailing.
- Freyr, the god of fertility, peace, and pleasure.
- Idun, the goddess of youth.

Odinist Theology

Odinists style themselves as life affirming, choosing to worship through feasting and "merrymaking." They do not see this life as a preparation for something better in another life, so they have no interest in fasting or acts of penitence.

The Odinist view is that life is a means unto itself – positive, good, hallowed, and to be enjoyed. The philosophy values anything that enriches and promotes life.

Although this attitude may sound materialistic, Odinists also recognize and honor the spiritual essence of man and the divine spark or soul that allows us to enter the halls of the gods and reunite with our ancestors.

For all their enjoyment of life, Odinists, like other neo-pagans recognize and seek balance between the material and spiritual realms.

Odinism is a nature religion with a strong emphasis on

identification with the qualities of the elements. Their principal deity, Odin, is the god of the wind and air. Frigg is associated with the land and the earth, Thor with lightning and thunder, and Niord with the sea and waves.

The Odinist philosophy is also animistic, holding that all beings including rivers, rocks, and mountains possess spiritual essence.

Rather that dividing creation into "heaven" and "earth," Odinist recognize multiple overlapping and enmeshed realms or dimension of reality.

The myths specifically speak of "Nine Worlds" across which cosmic conflicts are played out among opposing forces of nature.

According to the Odinist Fellowship website, this conflict

may be summarized as "the forces of Nature, order, life and creativity against the opposing forces of dissolution, disorder, disintegration and destruction."

Each man and woman chooses sides and plays their part in the conflict, thus finding the meaning of their life.

Odinist Ethics

Odinists are taught to cultivate the qualities of bravery and generosity. Although each branch of the faith may express these concepts in slightly different terms, the overall ethical nature of the belief is clear. This is a faith that is strongly based on concepts of personal honor and courage.
The Odinic Rite includes Nine Charges:

- courage
- truth
- honor
- fidelity
- discipline
- hospitality
- self-reliance
- industriousness
- perseverance

The Odin Brotherhood teaches "strength over weakness, pride over humility, and knowledge over faith."

By cultivating thoughtful practices, living a life of courage and honor, and fostering light and beauty, the members revere the gods.

Odinist Rites

New members who have reached the Age of Majority make a formal, public declaration of their beliefs by taking the Pledge of the Faith. The aspirant grasps the oath-ring while making their declaration.

(Oaths of all kinds are held to be sacred in Odinism.)

Subscribing to the "priesthood of all believers" any adult member who has made the Pledge of Faith can perform priestly duties and lead a congregation or group. There is, however, no requirement to do so.

Odinists have no "Bible," but adherents do honor the Eddas as primary sources of information. There are two Eddas, the Elder Edda and the Younger Edda, set down sometime in the 13th century. The books are collections of poetry and mythology.

The only form of "sacrifice" practiced by Odinists is a ritual called Sumbel in which a drinking horn of mead or ale is passed around participants gathered at a table.

Some of the mead is offered to the gods, and then each person who drinks makes a personal petition or pledges some form of a binding oath.

(Since drinking mead is the primary celebratory rite of Odinism, there has been a frank admission that in some groups, alcoholism is a problem. This is not encouraged by the faith, which, like other neo-pagan philosophies, teaches the princples of balance and moderation.)

Odinsit groups host outdoor celebrations of food and drink to honor the gods called blots. There are six major feast days including the solstices and Yule, Easter, Midsummer's Day, and the Harvest Festival.

Two other feast days are Sigurd's Day on April 23 and Einheriar (Heroe's day) on November 11. The first commemorates Sigurd, the dragon slayer, and the second honors the dead.

All feast days involve the ritualistic consumption of mead or ale.
Other Odinist ceremonies include Naming, which is akin to baptism in the Christian faith when water is poured over the head of newborn babies.

Weddings or Handfastings join couples and include the conventional exchange of finger fings. Both the bride and groom are blessed with the laying on of Thor's Hammer.

Funeral rites may or may not include cremation in the traditional Viking fashion.

Chapter 5 – Developing a Relationship with Deity

At least in the context of Western European tradition, pagan faiths not only worship a pantheon of gods, but also revere both the male and female principles.

In Wicca, for instance, we worship the Goddess and the God, or, as they are often called, the Lady and the Lord, but we have no issue with seekers who develop relationships with other deities.

All goddesses are part of the Lady, just as all gods are part of the Lord. Regardless of the names chosen for any aspect of the divine, deity itself is universal. For these reasons, it's not uncommon to hear the old gods referred to as The Nameless Ones.

Their voices come to us in different ways and with varying intensity. Every practitioner hears the gods and goddesses they are meant to hear. In addressing them in return and cultivating a relationship with them, you are finding your connection to the universal source.

An insistence on the superiority and ascendancy of the male principle only is an unbalanced and misogynistic aspect of Christianity that makes the religion too harsh and patriarchal for students of paganism.

We need the strong, male light of the sun by day, but the gentle, female rays of the moon balance him by night.

Balance and the Voice Within

The emphasis on balance in pagan pantheons allows us to temper the pull of opposing forces in our own journeys. Remember that anything taken to excess is seen as a negative.

I remember watching a woman on television once talking about her latest cookbook. The author, who was a public figure, had long been known for her struggles with weight.

The host of the show remarked that the author was looking quite well "these days," which was a polite euphemism for "thin." The woman smiled and said, "I finally learned that the best way to eat is to take all things in moderation, including moderation."

That was the principle of balance at work in her relationship with food. When she stopped following extreme diets that made her unhappy and emotionally unstable, her body responded in kind and shed the extra pounds.

All of life is full of these kinds of struggles, and in fact, the struggle itself is part of the problem. Spirituality that allows the practitioner to be free of dogmatic stereotypes associated with male and female roles liberates the individual to explore all aspects of their relationship not just with nature, but with themselves.

The exploration should be an effortless journey of curiosity, not a slog filled with struggle and strife.

Ignoring and thus dishonoring any kind of energy is not only unbalanced, it's unnatural. Self-help literature is replete with texts that talk about "the critical inner voice."

That's the voice that tells us we are unworthy, unlovable, unsuccessful, unredeemable, and a whole host of other "uns." If that is the only voice we allow to speak, then we live lives that do follow the dark side of negativity.

The Individual as Self-Priest

Paganism teaches us that we can speak with the gods because they are a part of us. When Martin Luther broke away from the Catholic Church and triggered the Protestant Reformation, he was actually echoing this old awareness.

Luther insisted that Christians could read the Bible for

themselves and they could intercede with the Christian God and develop a relationship with Him without the intermediary figure of a priest.

Luther was being quite pagan in his thinking whether he realized it or not. You will always be your own best intercessor -- your own priest or priestess. There is no barrier between you and the gods, so there is no cowering or begging for mercy or favor.

Our relationship with the gods is meant to be one of partnership and reciprocity founded on mutual respect for the universe we share.

When we talk to the gods, we are asking to find mental clarity to make right choices and to take right action in our daily lives. The pagan emphasis on personal responsibility is predicated on the individual's ability to read a situation and to follow the most beneficial and ethical path for themselves, for the community, and for the world.

Paganism is a strongly introspective way. We talk to the gods because they are our counselors and teachers, helping us to sort out the complexity of human existence and to find our proper and balanced place in the world.

Viewing the Gods

There are no injunctions on how you view the gods. For some people, seeing the deities as real personalities is helpful in cultivating a relationship with them.

Others are more comfortable seeing the deities as metaphors for universal principles like the archetypes developed by psychologist Carl Jung. It's perfectly alright to be playful and accepting as you work out your individual understanding.

Many years ago I was sitting with a friend who was filling out some sort of form. There was a box asking about religion, and she wrote, "Orthodox Druid." I asked if she would mind explaining that to me and with a smile she said, "Orthodox Druids pray to oak trees exclusively. Reform Druids will drop to their knees for any shrub they pass."

We both had a good laugh, and I suspect the deities laughed with us. Life is not meant to be such a very grim business. It's not my intention to keep laying the blame for downers at the feet of Christianity, but much of the theology of the last several hundred years in that church is predicated on the notion that you should suffer gracefully in this life in order to get something better in another life.

Certainly the concept of karma suggests that what you do in this life determines what you have to work out in the next one, but pagans frankly find the whole Christian idea of predestination and original sin more than a little harsh.

In a religious study group I once attended, a young woman threw up her hands in frustration over yet another round of "smiting" in the Old Testament and declared, "It's like every day was a bad hair day for God in this book!"

It is my personal belief that the Goddess and God have a sense of humor. We share many laughs over my personal foibles as I walk my path in life.

For me, my relationship with deity has to include laughter as a necessary counterpart to all the things that would seek to disturb the equilibrium of my life. I often find myself thinking that more laughter would benefit the whole world -- and with it, the whole universe.

What About the Idea of Evil?

I've already emphasized, several times, that pagans do not recognize the Christian concept of Satan, nor do they worship him. I've also touched on the idea that pagans do not envision the world as locked in a struggle between ultimate good and its counterpart in evil.

What pagans do recognize is that the universe is composed of opposites. Any one spirit can contain both good and bad qualities and so can the gods. All you have to do is spend a little time reading Greek and Roman mythology to find a pantheon where gods and goddesses do a fine job of getting themselves in trouble all the time.

Our ability to rise above those things in us that are "bad" is what prevents us from falling into a darker path. Pagan faiths emphasize the best qualities of the deities, but they do not gloss over those times when the gods make a mistake. Understanding divinity in this way makes the gods and goddesses much more accessible.

When you call out to a god or goddess to help you through an angry, painful time -- one that tempts you to take action that is not ethical, kind, or good -- the deity understands your hurt and your temptation. Like the wise counselors that they are, the gods help us get through those moments and find our true balance again.

The Many Pantheons

There are many groupings or pantheons of gods and goddesses from various traditions. You may be most familiar with those of the Greeks and Romans as they are often taught to high school students as part of lessons about the classical world.

The Greek pantheon includes:

- Aphrodite, the goddess of love, beauty, and sexuality.
- Apollo, the handsome god of the arts and of healing.
- Artemis, the goddess of the hunt and of the moon.
- Athena, the serious and beautiful goddess of wisdom.
- Demeter, the old woman who is goddess of the harvest.
- Dionysus, the god who embodies the force of life — and wine.
- Eros, the god of sexual attraction.
- Gaia, the nature and benevolent Mother Earth.
- Hades, the god of wealth and the underworld.
- Hecate, the goddess of the moon and of magic.
- Hera, the queen of the gods and consort of Zeus.

- Hermes, the god of travel, thought, and communication.
- Pan, the god of wild places and of shepherds.
- Persephone, the goddess of fertility, the spring, and the harvest.
- Poseidon, the god of the seas and of water.
- Zeus, the king of the gods and ruler of the skies.

The Roman pantheon includes:

- Ceres, the goddess of the harvest.
- Diana, the goddess of fertility and of the hunt.
- Fortuna, the goddess of fate and fortune.
- Janus, the god of doorways and beginnings.
- Juno, the goddess of the moon and of women.
- Jupiter, the king of the gods and ruler of the sky.
- Luna, the goddess of the moon.
- Mars, the god of agriculture and war.
- Mercury, the god of thought, communication, and travel.
- Neptune, the god of the seas and of water.
- Pluto, the god of wealth and the underworld.
- Venus, the goddess of beauty, love, and sexuality.

The members of any pantheon symbolize the complete elements of the given belief structure. The interaction of the gods and goddesses and the legends and beliefs associated with them teach valuable lessons and offer examples of both right and wrong conduct.

Remember, gods and goddesses are not always virtuous or correct! Sometimes the deities have as much or more to teach us from the mistakes they have made then from their strengths and accomplishments.

Pagans learn by not only studying the deeds of the gods, but also of developing personal relationships with them.

The neo-pagan movement of the last 300 years has displayed particular affinity for two pantheons, the Celtic gods and the Norse deities.

A short list of the many Celtic gods and goddesses includes:

- Alator, the Celtic god associated with war
- Belenus, the god of healing
- Bres, the god of fertility
- Brigantia, the goddess of river and water cults
- Brigit, the goddess of fire, fertility, healing, and poetry
- Ceridwen, the keeper of the cauldron of wisdom
- Epona, the goddess of horses who accompies souls on their final journey
- Latobius, the god of mountains and sky
- Lugh, the god of craftsmen
- Maponus, the god of music and poetry
- Morrigan, the goddess of war
- Nehalennia, the goddess of seafarers
- Nemausicaw, the mother goddess of healing and fertility

The Norse pantheon is also extensive. The major gods and goddesses include, but are not limited to:

- Baldur - God of beauty, innocence, peace, and rebirth.
- Borr - Father of Óðinn, Vili and Ve.
- Bragi - God of poetry, music and the harp.
- Búri - The first god\.
- Dagur - God of the daytime.
- Delling - God of dawn.
- Eir - Goddess of healing.
- Ēostre - Goddess of spring.
- Elli - Goddess of old age.
- Forseti - God of justice, peace and truth.
- Freyja - Goddess of love, fertility, and battle.
- Freyr - God of fertility.
- Frigg - Goddess of marriage and motherhood.
- Gefjun - Goddess of fertility and plough.
- Hel - Queen of Helheim, the Norse underworld.
- Hermóður - The heroic son of Odin.
- Hlín - Goddess of consolation and protection.
- Höðr - God of winter.
- Hœnir - The silent god.
- Iðunn - Goddess of youth.
- Jörð - Goddess of the Earth.
- Kvasir - God of inspiration.
- Lofn - Goddess of forbidden loves.
- Loki - Trickster and god of mischief.
- Magni - God of strength.
- Máni - God of the Moon.
- Nanna - Goddess of joy and peace.
- Njörður - God of sea, wind, fish, and wealth..
- Nótt - Goddess of night.
- Óðinn - The "All Father" God of war, associated with wisdom, poetry, and magic.

- Rán - Goddess of the sea.
- Sif - Wife of Thor. Goddess of harvest.
- Sjöfn - Goddess of love.
- Skaði - Goddess of winter.
- Snotra - Goddess of prudence.
- Sol (Sunna) - Goddess of the Sun.
- Thor - God of thunder and battle.
- Týr - God of war.
- Ullr - God of winter, hunts, and duels.
- Váli - God of revenge.
- Vár - Goddess of contracts.
- Víðarr - God of the forest, revenge and silence.
- Vör - Goddess of wisdom.

Don't think that because you have chosen to follow a pagan path that you are limited to developing relationship with the European or classical pantheons.

I know practicing Wiccans who also venerate members of the Hindu pantheon after coming to a spiritual awareness of the influence of these deities through the practice of yoga and various meditation techniques.

Always hold yourself open to the voices of the gods. Pay attention to how they may be speaking to you. The saying that there are no coincidences is quite true.

You may be sitting on an airplane and casually take in the title of the book your seat mate is reading. For some reason, the title simply will not leave your thoughts.

That's how signs come to us. Quietly. Go to a bookstore,

find a copy of the volume, and read a few pages. You may find that there is material there you need to help you along the next stage of your journey.

Chapter 6 – Pagan Symbols

The study of symbolism is a fascinating pursuit and one that can help you to find spiritual elements you might not otherwise discover. If you find yourself powerfully drawn to a symbol inscribed on an amulet or a piece of jewelry, investigate why the image is reaching out to you.

Long before I became a pagan, I was deeply drawn to Celtic imagery especially that connected with Scottish mythology. Now, having done past life work and spending time in the highlands of Scotland, I understand that in a past life, those mountains were my home.

The Celtic symbols with their elegant knots and intricate meanings continue to speak to me more eloquently than any other pagan symbols and I have many fine examples of Celtic amulets in my home.

Symbolic jewelry allows pagans to infuse their daily lives with subtle magic. To the casual observer, the ring on your hand may be nothing more than an attractive piece of jewelry. To you, it symbolizes a powerful bridge between the material and spiritual worlds.

The following symbols are some of the most common in pagan spirituality, but they barely scratch the surface of the wealth of emblems employed by the various faiths. In this regard, the Internet is a wonderful resource for the beginning pagan. Search for phrases like "Pagan amulets" or "Celtic charms." You will find not only beautiful items for purchase, but useful explanations of the symbols.

Pentacle

The five-pointed star or pentacle is one of the most widely recognized of all pagan symbols. This emblem has nothing to do with Satanic worship and it is not a symbol of the devil.

The four points of the star represent the traditional elements of earth, water, air, and fire with the fifth honoring spirit.

The circle connecting the points denotes the reciprocal relationship of the elements as they are embodied in nature.

Pentacles are used in magical work and are placed on altars in various traditions. Since the emblem is one of protection, pentacles are also popular as amulets and other pieces of jewelry.

Triquatra

Both Christians and pagans use the triquatra or "trinity knot." The symbol dates to the 7th century A.D. and in neo-paganism is specific to The Morrígan, a triple goddess associated with war.

In some traditions, especially in modern times, the triquatra is a symbol of the intimate connection of mind, body, and soul. It is popular with many Celtic pagan groups who use it as an emblem of the earth, sea, and sky.

The triquatra is one of the simplest of the Celtic knots, which may account for its popularity. The graceful lines and balance of the symbol are appealing and its triple nature lends itself to multiple interpretations.

Chalice

The cup or chalice is both a symbol and a tool in pagan ritual. It represents water and the feminine aspects of intuition, psychic ability, emotions, and the subconscious. The cup also depicts fertility and gestation and is an emblem of the womb of the Goddess.

Like other pagan symbols, the chalice also has strong Christian associations, especially those associated with the Holy Grail – the cup used at the Last Supper, which then caught the blood of Jesus spilled from the cross.

Interestingly enough, the Grail myth is believed to have been adapted from older Celtic tails of maidens who guarded sacred wells.

Triskele

The triskele, which can be found carved in Neolithic stones in Ireland and Western Europe, is an emblem of the realms of the earth, sea, and sky.

Although its origins pre-date the Celtic peoples, the triskele is popular with Celtic neo-pagans as well as some Germanic groups. Like the triquatra, this symbol is useful to depict any triple concepts.

The symbol is so common it appears in such incongruous places as the seal of the United States Department of Transportation and (in roundel form) on the emblem of the Irish Air Corps. Many Christian churches incorporate the triskele in carvings and stained glass windows.

Four Elements

Each of the four classical elements of earth, water, air, and fire has a representative symbol used in pagan ritual and adornment.

The air symbol, for instance, is an emblem of the connection between the breath of life and the soul. The triangles are simple to work into jewelry designs and are often used in concert with other symbols as bounding devices.

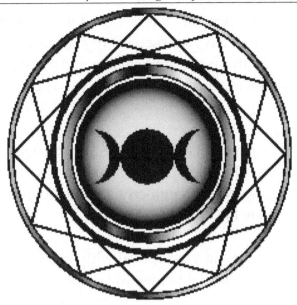

Triple Moon

The triple moon symbol depicts the three phases of the moon (waxing, full, waning). It is sometimes referred to as the triple goddess symbol, reflecting the three phases of a woman's life (maiden, mother, crone.)

The waxing moon represents new life, new beginnings, and rejuvenation. The full moon is the manifestation of magic at its most powerful point. The waning moon represents the sending away or removal of things in your life or the need to finish something left incomplete.

Caring for Your Pagan Symbols

When you wear symbols of your pagan faith on your body, the jewelry absorbs the energies moving through your system.

In a sense of "attunement" this is a good thing. There are times, however, when your own energy needs to be "re-charged." Once this is accomplished, you don't want to then be exposed to any stored negativity in your symbolic objects.

I like to take my amulets and energetically cleanse them at least once a month, especially it it's during a period when I have been grappling with numerous problems and challenges in my life.

If the symbol is strongly associated with female energy, I place the items in the light of the full moon. If their energy is more masculine, they go into a warm, energizing puddle of sunlight.

With new jewelry, it's best to first cleanse the pieces under running water before wearing them. This removes any negative energy that has entered the items through casual content.

While the jewelry is submerged in the water, offer a cleansing prayer. After a minute or so, take the items out and gently pat them dry.

To charge the jewelry and make it your own, wear it against your skin for 7-9 days. This binds the piece to you. Avoid letting anyone else touch or handle the item.

If this is unavoidable, immediately cleanse the piece in moonlight or sunlight.

Personally, I also have an attraction to antique jewelry. I often find that these pieces "speak" to me in powerful ways. If you do acquire any item of jewelry, especially one with symbolic significance that has been worn by another person, take the time to cleanse and recharge the item.

This will not lessen your psychic connection to the piece, but it will protect your from any stored, latent energies that might affect you in a negative way.

Chapter 7 – Pagan Terminology

Again, there are whole dictionaries written to explain the specific terms used in pagan spirituality. The following sampling should be of use as you begin to explore more detailed texts explaining pagan belief.

Adept - A person killed in the practice of magic or mysticism.

Air - One of the classic elements in Western paganism.

Altar - A flat surface reserved exclusively for the working of Magick that is utilized as a focus of power.

Amulet - An object charged with Magick for the deflection of specific negative energies. A protective object.

Animism - The belief that all of creation is alive, even objects perceived to be inanimate.

Asperger - A perforated object or bundle of fresh herbs used during or preceding a Ritual to sprinkle water for purposes of purification.

Association - The correlation or connection of two or more idea, beings, or objects to create a pattern.

Astral plane - The spiritual or nonphysical plane.

Astral projection - To separate the consciousness and the physical body so that the consciousness might move at will.

Athame - A double-edged blade with a black handed used by Wiccans as a ritual knife for the direction of Personal Power. Seldom, if ever, used to actually make a physical cut. The origin of the term is obscure and there are many variant spellings.

Balefire - Fires lit for Magickal purposes in an outdoor setting. Traditionally used at Yule, Beltane and Midsummer.

Bane - Something that is destructive, evil, dangerous, or poisonous. Destroys life.

Beltane - Also known as May Eve, Roodmas, Walpurgis Night, or Cethsamhain, this Wiccan festival is celebrated on either April 30 or May 1 depending on the tradition. It commemorates the symbolic joining (matting or marriage) of the Goddess and God. An anticipation of the coming months of summer.

Besom - A witch's broom, used to purify spaces. Typically made of either willow or birch.

Blessing - Magic used for the purpose of bringing benefit to a person, object, or space.

Blue Moon - The second of two full moons in one calendar month.

Bolline - A white-handled knife used by Wiccans for practical purposes in magick like cutting herbs.

Book of Shadows - A Wiccan's Book of Shadows is a workbook and repository for a witch's notes, rituals, spells, and other workings. Alternately called a Grimoire. Traditionally handwritten, but may be kept in any form factor.

Burning Times - A reference to periods of witch persecution in the Middle Ages or Medieval Period and later.

Calling the Quarters - The symbolic or verbal acknowledgement of Earth, Air, Fire, and water (The Four Elements) in a ritual setting.

Cartomancy - A system of divination by the use of Tarot cards.

Casting a Circle - The creation of an encircling Magickal sphere around a ritual working space to enhance focus and raise and contain power until the energy is ready to be released

Casting Runes - A system of divination that makes use of small stones inscribed with runic letters.

Cauldron - A three-legged pot, traditionally made of cast-iron to hold fire or candles, to burn incense, or to make brews. The cauldron is representative of the Self and serves as a point of transformation.

Centering - The meditative exercise of centering is preceded by grounding and is designed to achieve total calm in the body for the maximum flow of energy and a sense of being one with the Universe.

Censer - A container for the burning of incense that symbolizes the Element of Air.

Chalice - A ritualistic cup used in ritual as a representation of the Goddess. It is a symbol of potential.

Charge - The act of Magick that infuses Personal Power into an object.

Clan - A group of any number of covens that are in agreement to follow a given set of rules under a single leader.

Conscious Mind - The rational half of the human consciousness that is materially based and analytical.

Correspondence - An item with Magickal association to hours, days, moon phases, planets, oils, herbs, colors, gemstones, and the like.

Coven - A Wiccan group that typically has an initiatory process and is under the leadership of one or two people.

Covenstead - A coven's regular meeting place or home.

Craft - An alternate name for Wicca and Witchcraft.

Crescent Moon - The sacred symbol of the Goddess that is used in invocations, women's healings, and during Sabbats.

Crystal ball - Crystal balls are actually made of quartz, which is cold to the touch and includes unique irregularities. A device for divination.

Crystallomancy - A system of divination that uses spheres of glass or quartz.

Curse - A curse is cast by directing negative energy at someone purposely. Their use is NOT sanctioned by the Wiccan faith.

Dagger - A knife used in ritual to sever psychic bonds among other functions.

Dedication - The ritual whereby an individual accepts Wicca (The Craft) as their life path and is then considered to be a reborn child of the Goddess and God.

Deity - A powerful being or essence perceived by pagans to be a part of or to infuse all of the spirit of the universe.

Deosil - Pronounced "jess-el," this is a clockwise motion that mimics the perceived direction of the sun in the sky. In the northern hemisphere, deosil movement in rituals symbolizes life and positive energy. Some groups below the equator use widdershin or counter-clockwise motion as the sun appears to move in that fashion from their geographic vantage point.

Divination - A magickal art of contacting the psychic mind to discover the unknown. This is achieved through the ritualistic manipulation of tools like tarot cards or a crystal ball or by discerning random patterns in materials like tea leaves or smoke.

Divine Power - The pure energy, life force, and ultimate source of all things that exists within the Goddess and God.

Drawing Down the Moon – A ritual to connect with the Goddess on the Full Moon by drawing her spirit down into an individual, either a Priestess or a sole practitioner.

Druid - The warrior / priest class of the ancient Celtic peoples whose philosophies and functions as healers, diplomats, judges, historians, musicians, poets, and intellectuals has been revived over the past 300 years in the Neo-Pagan.

Earth - One of the classic elements in Western paganism.

Earth Power - The Divine Power that manifests in natural objects like herbs, flames, sones, or even the wind. It can be used during Magick as a means of creating needed change.

Elements - The four elements are Earth, Air, Fire, and Water. These building blocks of the Universe are contained singly or in combination (or as potential) in everything that exists. They can be used during Magick and are formed from the primal power known as Akasha.

Esbat - An esbat occurs when a coven or an individual witch ritualistically celebrates the Full Moon. These observances are different than sabbats, which celebrate the seasons of the year.

Evocation - The calling up of any non-physical entity including spirits to be in visible or invisible attendance.

Familiars - The pets of witches that have been trained to serve as Magickal helpers.

Fire - One of the classic elements in Western paganism.

Goddess and God - The terms for the universal male and female deities that are celebrated by Wicca as the equal and polar halves of The All.

Great Rite - The Great Rite is a form of sexual magick that can include actual intercourse or the symbolic representation of the act by lowering the athame into the chalice.

Grimoire - Also known as a Book of Shadows, a grimoire is a witch's notebook. Modern grimoires are kept as a repository of personal ritual and Magickal information, but many grimoires from the 16th and 17th century are famous works that include not only formulae for spells, but also catalogs of spirits.

Grounding - Grounding is an exercise in meditation that allows the practitioner to draw or send energy into the Earth.

Handfasting - The term for a Wiccan wedding.

Imbolc - The Wiccan festival celebrating the first signs of spring. It is celebrated on February 2 and is also known as

Candlemas, Lupercalia, Feast of Pan, Feast of Torches, Feast of the Waxing Light, Oimelc, and Brigit's Day among others.

Initiation - The introduction or admission of an individual into a coven by a ritual occasion or a spontaneous Invocation.

Infusion - A liquid that is made by soaking herbs in hot water.

Invocation - The method of causing the God or Goddess to appear by establishing conscious ties to them through awareness of their dwelling within each of us.

Labrys - In ancient Crete this double-headed axe was a symbol for the Goddess. It is still used for this purpose in Wicca today, and may be placed or leaned against the left side of the altar.

Lughnasadh - Celebrated on August 1, this Wiccan festival is also known as August Eve, Lammas, Feast of Bread. It marks the first harvest.

Lady - Alternate title of honor for the Goddess.

Lord - Alternate title of honor for the God.

Mabon - Wiccans celebrate the second harvest on or around the autumn equinox, which is typically close to September 21. It is a recognition of nature preparing to enter winter.

Magick - Creating needed change by the movement of natural energies like Personal Power or by building or rousing the energy that exists in colors, plants, stones, sounds or movements and then release it. This is a little understood natural process, and is not "supernatural." The spelling "Magick" is used intentionally to distinguish real magick from stage magic.

Magick Circle - Often called simply the "Circle," this is a sphere of Personal Power unwise which rituals are enacted. It is created through both visualization and the use of Magick, typically with the Athame, a wand, or the fingers.

Meditation - The contemplative practice of focusing inward on the self and personal power or outward on the Deity and nature for grounding and centering. May be assisted by particular thoughts or symbols as points of focus.

Midsummer - The Wiccan festival held at the summer solstice, which is usually on or near June 21st. It is the time of the year when the Sun and thus the God is believed to be at the height of its powers, and is also the longest day of the year.

Mundane Plane – The daily physical plane on which we all exist.

Neo-Pagan - Any member of the newly revived Pagan or earth religions that are once again gaining popularity around the world. All Wiccans are, by definition pagan, but it does not follow that all pagans are Wiccans.

Old Ones - This term is sometimes used as an all-encompassing reference to the Gddess and God in all their aspects.

Ostara - The Wiccan observance of the spring equinox that typically occurs around March 21st. It marks the advent of spring and is a festival of fire and fertility.

Pagan - The term for followers of all polytheistic, shamanistic, and Magickal religions including Wicca.

Pendulum - A device of divination that is comprised of some type of heavy object attached to a string or chain. The free end of the string is held in the user's hand, elbow resting on a flat surface. As questions are asked, the movement of the object is used to indicate yes or no answers. A tool used to make contact with the Psychic Mind.

Pentacle - Pentacles are any circular objects including jewelry on which a Pentagram has been inscribed.

Personal Power - The energy that originates with the Goddess and God and sustains our bodies. Working Magick involves moving personal power in the direction of achieving a specific goal.

Phases of the Moon - The phases of the moon as it journeys around the Earth are waxing, full, and waning.

Polarity - Any energy that is opposite but equal. For instance, hot and cold or yin and yang. Wicca recognizes the polarity inherent in deity as the feminine and masculine principles embodied in the Goddess and God.

Psychic Mind - That portion of the mind with which we receive psychic impulses, also known as the subconscious or unconscious mind. The psychic mind is at work during sleeping, dreaming, and meditation.

Reincarnation - The rebirth or repeated incarnation of spirit into physical, human form.

Ritual - A ceremony involving specific movements and/or manipulation of objects for the purpose of achieving union with an aspect of the divine. In the working of Magick, a ritual produces a particular state of consciousness that enables the movement of energy toward a goal.

Runes - The stick-like figures that are remnants of old Teutonic alphabets and pictographs. Typically inscribed on stones for purposes of divination.

Sabbat - Any one of the Wiccan festivals of Beltane, Imbolc, Lughnasadh, Mabon, Midsummer, Ostara, Samhain and Yule.

Sacred Space - Any area that has been consecrated and cleansed for the purpose of performing ritual or working Magick.

Samhain - The Wiccan festival celebrated on October 31. Also known as November Eve, Hallowmas, Halloween, the Feast of Souls, the Feast of the Dead, of the Feast of Apples.

Scry - The act of gazing into or at an object to contact the psychic mind for purposes of divination. Objects used may include a quartz crystal sphere, a pool of water, reflections, or a candle flame.

Shaman - A man or woman who, through periods of alternate consciousness, has pierced the veil of the physical world and experienced the realm of energies, thus gaining the power to change the world through the use of Magick.

"So Mote It Be" - An expression that means, "As I will, so it will be."

Spell - A ritual for Magick purposes that is not religious and involves the use of spoken words.

Talisman - An object charged with power to attract specific energy to its bearer, such as an amethyst crystal.

Tarot Cards - A set of 78 cards used for purposes of divination.

The All - The primary energy of the universe. Its polarities are represented by the Goddess and God.

Tradition - A specific subgroup of the Wiccan belief that practices unique variations of the rituals of the Craft.

Visualization - The process of forming mental images to achieve needed goals during ritual or the working of Magick.

Walpurgis Night (Walpurgisnacht) – A traditional festival held on April 30 or May 1 each year in large parts of Northern and Central Europe. The occasion is marked with bonfires and dancing. The literal translation from the German is "Witches Night."

Wand - A piece of wood typically one foot in length that is used to invoke the deities and to channel energy.

Waning Moon - The phase of the moon between a full moon and a new or waxing moon.

Water - One of the classic elements in Western paganism.

Waxing Moon - The phase of the moon preceding a full moon.

Wheel of the Year -- One full cycle of the Wiccan year comprised of eight seasons each celebrated with a Sabbat.

White-Handled Knife - A knife used for utilitarian purposes by Wiccans like cutting up herbs. Often called a bolline.

Wicca - A pagan contemporary religion with roots in Shamanism, that reveres the Goddess and God, and emphasizes ritual observance and the practice of Magick.

Widdershins - Anti-clockwise motion used in Wicca for ritualistic purposes. The opposite of Deosil.

Witch - A practitioner of pre-Christian folk magick,

particularly that relating to herbs, healing, wells, rivers and stones.

Yule - The Wiccan festival celebrated on or around December 21 that marks the rebirth of the Sun God from the Earth Goddess. Occurs on the Winter Solstice.

Yggdrasil – Derived from Norse mythology, this is one of the best-known Tree of Life symbols, illustrating the united existence of the underworld and the physical world.

Chapter 8 - Simple Rituals for Beginners

If you opt to follow a tradition and to join a pagan group, you will be instructed in the rites associated with their regular activities. Many pagan traditions have a master / apprentice form of teaching that is especially tailored for this purpose.

This does not mean, however, that you will not want to incorporate personal rituals into your own daily activities. These observances will come to you naturally as you study and become attuned to the deities with whom you have an affinity.

The following simply practices, however, can help the beginning practitioners to feel more protected and focused as they begin to walk the pagan path.

Smudging

Smudging is a simple ritual common to many pagan traditions. The purpose of the rite is to cleanse an area of negative energy or energy that has become stagnant. Many people like to perform such a cleansing when they move into a new home, for instance, or seasonally as a kind of spiritual "spring cleaning."

The preferred tool is a bundle of sage, but other fragrant herbs like lavender or sweetgrass may be used, and even incense is acceptable. You may even choose to mix lavender in with your bundle of sage because the fragrance it leaves behind is so pleasant and energizing.

Begin by lighting a candle and taking a moment to focus your energy. Offer a prayer to the deity of your choice, then light the bundle of sage and allow it to flame for a few seconds before blowing it out.

The bundle will continue to smoke. Move throughout the space to be cleansed in a clockwise motion gently waving the bundle to disperse the smoke. Spend a little extra time in the corners where energy tends to gather and stagnate.

If you are concerned about working with a smouldering bundle, place the sage in a fireproof bowl and disperse the smoke with your hand or with a feather.

When the area has been thoroughly smudged, return to the point at which you began and extinguish the bundle of sage in a bowl of clean sand.

If you so desire, allow the candle to continue to burn as a focal point for good energy to come into the space.

You can also use smudging to clear negative energy from your own body or from that of another person. Begin at the soles of the feet and direct the cleansing smoke upward over the legs, torso, and upper body, finishing in the area above the head.

Candle Magic

Candle magic is a simple ritual for beginners since nothing is required in terms of equipment. Even people who do not follow a pagan path use candles on ceremonial occasions from elegant weddings to candles on a birthday cake.

Candles help the practitioner to focus and to direct their will, desires, and concerns.

Select a plain candle with a clean, uniform shape. You do not want a candle that distracts from your ability to concentrate.

The candle should be new and not secondhand. As you become more conversant with corollary magical tools like essential oils, you may want to add a few drops to the flame to further concentrate your will.

Select a color that suggests the outcome your desire:

- *white* - All purpose and excellent as a general mediation tool.

- *black* - Protection against retribution from a party feeling wronged. Also used in banishing rituals. (That isn't as ominous as it might sound. You might just want to "banish" the negativity you are feeling over your new boss at work.)

- *blue* - A color of peace and harmony that promotes protection and healing, the mending of friendships, the breaking of bad habits, and clearing of the air after arguments or discord.

- *brown* - A grounding color that aids in stabilization. Brown candles are excellent when you want to achieve better balance or seek justice in a situation.

- *gold / light yellow* - This is a color that attracts positive cosmic influences and can bring about good luck, including financial gain.

- *green* - Green is a color often used to clear obstacles and to reveal hidden treasure. It is used to bring material success and to promote generosity and healing (especially with regard to "female" problems.)

- *indigo / magenta* - These deeply hued candles create high vibrational frequencies and are useful in getting fast and definitive changes.

- *orange* - Orange is an excellent choice for people who need to find a new job, are in need of encouragement, or who need to communicate with someone at a distance.

- *pink* - This color is good for all magic associated with love, romance, and the healing of couples.

Designing Your Own Ritual

Remember that you are perfectly free to design your own rituals, and are, in fact, encouraged to do so. The more that you can create spiritual practices that actually fit into your daily life, the more likely you will be to actually live and observe your pagan faith. Here are a few tips to help you get started.

Create a ritual space.

Personally, I am drawn to small, minimalist spaces. I have converted a corner of my bedroom for ritual purpose by setting up a simple table to serve as an altar. I rarely use tools beyond candles and my favorite crystals.

I am especially drawn to black onyx, which is often called the "Stone of Self-Mastery." Onyx is a healing, grounding, and protective stone. It is so useful in blocking negative influences that I even wear a silver ring set with a simple piece of onyx.

I keep a larger piece of onyx on my altar, positioned so that it reflects the flickering flame of my candle when it is lit. The effect is hypnotic, and especially good for meditative work.

Tiger's Eye is also a favorite. This "Stone of the Mind" is also centering, grounding, and protective, but also stimulates creativity and promotes balance. I keep Tiger's Eye on my altar because it improves clear thinking and enhances insight.

Writing your ritual.

Explore your motivation for conducting the ritual and spend some time writing down all the words you want to use and the order in which you want to complete the steps.

For instance, you might write down:

1. Center your energy.
2. Light a candle in the color appropriate to your intent.
3. Purify the space with sage.
4. Invoke the presence of a god or goddess.
5. Raise your power through meditation.
6. State your intention / request.
7. Thank the deity for their presence.
8. Spend a few minutes in quiet contemplation.
9. Extinguish the candle.

Once you have worked out the steps of your ritual, you may opt to actually do the work within the safety of a magic circle.

Casting a Circle

A circle is cast for the purpose of containing undirected energies, concentrating your energy, and protecting yourself from energies outside your working space. Think of the circle as a protective bubble or sphere surrounding you on all sides.

Do not attempt to cast a circle when you are:

- ill
- exhausted
- unfocused
- ill-prepared
- angry

Always fill your circle with positive energy. To cast a circle:

Cleanse your working space of all negativity. Wiccans use a broom, but smudging will also work.

Consecrate the space either by lighting a candle and praying or by circling the area three times in a clockwise direction carrying first a bowl of pure water, then a bowl or salt, and thean a stick of burning incense.

Next, using a ritual device like a wand or staff, trace the edge of the circle while walking clockwise and envisioning the power pulling itself up to cloak and surround you.

Taking Down the Circle

When your ritual is finished, take down your circle by thanking the deities you've asked to be present and then by addressing and thanking the four points of the compass.

Using the same implement that was employed to draw the circle, "undraw" it by moving in a counterclockwise position, letting down the energy as you move. Think of the energy as leaving your body and flowing back into the earth.

You may wish to finish this procedure by saying, "The circle is open, but never broken."

In Wiccan coven work, the leader will then invite all spirits who have been drawn to the power created to go on their way by saying, "May all beings and elementals attracted to this ritual be on their way harming one."

The members then respond with, "Merry ye meet, and merry ye part, and merry ye meet again.

Use a Journal or Book of Shadows

Over time, you will refine and extend your rituals. For this reason, and as a personal record of your deepening journey, I recommend keeping a journal or book of shadows. The longer you follow this practice, the more the book will become a working part of your spiritual life. For most pagans, their Book of Shadows is a deeply personal, sacred possession.

Afterword

Here at the end of my text, I think the reader will understand that I am personally drawn to the path of a sole practitioner. That stems largely from negative experiences with organized religion early in my life.

I came to paganism initially out of a deep and abiding connection with nature and because I found great personal freedom in the idea of discovering and crafting my own spiritual path in life.

The ethical and ecumenical tone of Wicca spoke to me, and, although the faith worships the Lady and the Lord equally, Wicca is a strongly feminist faith.

Although I am not a member of a coven, I do have many women friends who are also followers of a Wicca and I do feel part of a "sisterhood" of Wiccan witches.

All of these elements answered my spiritual needs and helped me to begin to form better questions about my role in the world. The pagan principles of balance and ethical action quickly became my touchstones.

At conferences and workshops, however, I met many other kinds of pagans. I do confess that the first practicing Druid I encountered was at a Renaissance Faire and he was dressed as a stereotypical wizard complete with gray robe, white beard, and pointed hat.

Over several mugs of good ale, however, he began to talk to

me about the Druid way of life. We quickly found common ground in our shared veneration of nature, and I enjoyed listening to his descriptions of perceived tribal connections extending backward into the Iron Age.

In the final analysis, I think many pagans are searchers in a modern and increasingly technological world. We do not want to lose the song of the forest and the field. We do not want the magic of nature to disappear in the current of the circuit and the microchip.

We recognize that mankind is causing grave harm to Mother Earth and her creatures, and we are answering the call in whatever way we can to help heal our planet and foster a new age of environmental responsibility.

My Druid friend is part of a group that goes out every weekend and plants trees. I have spent more than one Saturday wielding a shovel with them. I always feel the Lady and the Lord smiling at our efforts.

My friend calls the saplings his Brothers and I do get a real sense of family connection when the scattered lot of us with our shovels and gloves and shared belief in something greater than ourselves.

Sometimes those days end with a bonfire and good tales from a bard in the group, singing and music, or just quiet conversation as we stare into the elemental flames.

To be pagan is to be connected within and without. All paths are valid, and you will find your own way. This book has been intended merely as an introduction to a different way of viewing spirituality. I cannot tell you which path to take, nor would I presume to try.

I will tell you that in your journey, experiences are as crucial as reading and studying. Even as a sole practitioner, I try to spend time with others who share my worldview. This does often occur in settings like Renaissance Faires, but I also am a regular at a wonderful metaphysical bookstore where customers engage in lively conversation over steaming cups of the proprietor's wonderful teas.

More than anything, the pagan way is one that calls on the seeker to live life and in the living to learn. I wish you good speed on your journey and, "Merry meet, and merry part, until we merry meet again."

Suggested Reading

Adler, Margot. *Drawing Down the Moon: Witches, Druids, Goddess-Worshippers, and Other Pagans in America*. Penguin Books, 2006.

Albertsson, Alaric. *To Walk a Pagan Path: Practical Spirituality for Every Day*. Llewellyn Publications, 2013.

Andrews, Lynn V. *Medicine Woman*. San Francisco: Harper & Row, 1981.

Baring, Anne, and Jules Cashford. *The Myth of the Goddess: Evolution of an Image*. London: Penguin, 1991.

Beyerl, Paul. *A Compendium of Herbal Magick*. Custer, WA: Phoenix Publishing, 1998.

Blake, Deborah. *Circle, Coven & Grove: A Year of Magickal Practice*. Deborah Blake, 2014.

Blake, Deborah. *Everyday Witchcraft: Making Time for Spirit in a Too-Busy World*. Llewellyn Publications, 2015.

Brogan, Stuart. *Heathen Warrior*. Midgard, 2013.

Buckland, Raymond. *Buckland's Complete Book of Witchcraft*. St. Paul: Llewellyn Publications, 1985.

Campbell, Joseph. *The Masks of God: Creative Mythology*. New York: Viking Press, 1971.

Campbell, Joseph. *The Power of Myth*. New York: Doubleday, 1988.

Chappel, Helen. *The WaxingMoon: A Gentle Guide to Magick*. New York: Links, 1974.

Coyle, T. Thorn. *Crafting a Daily Practice*. Sunna Press, 2012.

Crowley, Vivianne. *Way of Wicca*. London: Thorsons, 1997.

Cunningham, Scott. *Wicca: A Guide for the Solitary Practitioner*. St. Paul, MN: Llewellyn, 1989.

Cunningham, Scott. *Cunningham's Encyclopedia of Crystal, Gem, and Metal Magick*. St. Paul, MN: Llewellyn Publications, 1993.

Cunningham, Scott. *Cunningham's Encyclopedia of Magickal Herbs*. St. Paul, MN: Llewellyn Publications, 1985.

Curott, Phyllis. *Book of Shadows: A Modern Woman's Journey into the Wisdom of Witchcraft and the Magick of the Goddess*. New York: Broadway/Random House, 1998.

Eason, Cassandra. *A Complete Guide to Faeries & Magical Beings: Explore the Mystical Realm of the Little People*. Weiser Books, 2002.

Farrar, Janet and Stewart Farrar. *Eight Sabbats for Witches*. London: Robert Hale, 1981.

Farrar, Janet and Stewart Ferrar. *A Witches' Bible: The*

Complete Witches' Handbook. Custer, WA: Phoenix Publishing, 1981.

Gardner, Gerald. The Meaning of Witchcraft. London: 1959. London: Aquarian Press, 1971.

Graves, Robert. The White Goddess. New York: Farrar, Straus and Giroux, 1973.

Heselton, Philip. Gerald Gardner and the Cauldron of Inspiration. Somerset, England: Capall Bann, 2003.

Heselton, Philip. Wiccan Roots: Gerald Gardner and the Modern Witchcraft Revival. Somerset, England: Capall Bann, 2000.

Higginbotham, River and Joyce Higginbotham. Paganism: An Introduction to Earth-Centered Religions. Llewellyn Publications, 2002.

Howells, William. The Heathens: Primitive Man and His Religions. Garden City (New York): Doubleday, 1956.

K., Amber. Covencraft: Witchcraft for Three or More. St. Paul, MN: Llewellyn Publications, 1998.
Leek, Sybil. The Complete Art of Witchcraft. New York: World Publishing, 1971.

Kreeft, Peter and Blaise Pascal. Christianity for Modern Pagans. Ignatius Press, 1993.

Lafaylive, Patrica M. A Practical Heathen's Guide to Asatru.

Llewellyn Publications, 2013.

MommaWhiteCougar The Pagan. *The Sacred Wheel: A Guide to the Pagan Year for Beginners in Witchcraft and Wicca.* New Age & Spiritual Books, 2012.

O'Donnell, James J. *Pagans: The End of Traditional Religion and the Rise of Christianity.* Ecco, 2015.

Sabin, Thea. *Wicca for Beginners: Fundamentals of Philosophy and Practice.* St. Paul, MN: Llewellyn, 2006.

Sentier, Elen. *Shaman Pathways – Trees of the Goddess: A New Way of Working with the Ogham.* Moon Books, 2014.

Serith, Ceisiwr. *A Book of Pagan Prayer.* Weiser Books, 2002.

Starhawk. *The Spiral Dance: a Rebirth of the Ancient Religion of the Great Goddess.* San Francisco: Harper and Row, 1979.

Valiente, Doreen. *An ABC of Witchcraft Past and Present.* New York: St. Martin's, 1973.

van der Hoeven, Joanna. *Pagan Portals – The Awen Alone: Walking the Path of the Solitary Druid.* Moon Books, 2014.

Weinstein, Marion. *Earth Magick: A Dianic Book of Shadows.* New York: Earth Magick Productions, 1980.

Weinstein, Marion. *Positive Magick: Occult Self-Help.* New York: Pocket Books, 1978.
Worth Valerie. *The Crone's Book of Words.* St. Paul: St. Paul,

MN: Llewellyn Publications, 1971, 1986.

Zimmerman, Denise, and Katherine A. Gleason. *The Complete Idiots Guide to Wicca and Witchcraft*. Indianapolis, IN: Alpha Books, 2000.

Online Resources

Like all online sources, I cannot guarantee that these sites will be in operation when you attempt to access them, but all were in business at the time of this writing in mid-2015.

13Moons
www.13moons.com

Ancient Order of Druids in America
www.aoda.org

AzureGreen
www.azuregreen.net

Bellirosa's Needful Things
www.bellirosa.com

Brighton Wiccan Supplies
brightonwiccansupplies.co.uk

The Caluldrom: A Pagan Forum
www.ecauldron.com

Eclectic Artisans
www.eartisans.net

Internet Sacred Text Archive
www.-sacred-texts.com

Isis Books and Gifts
www.isisbooks.com

Moon Aria
www.moonaria.com

Moon's Light Magic
www.moonslightmagic.com

Mystickal Arts Treasures
www.mystickalartstreasures.com

Occult Wiccan Supply Shop
www.paganstuffcheap.com

The Odinist Fellowship
www.odinistfellowship.co.uk

Order of Bards, Ovates, and Druids
www.druidry.org

Pagan Federation International - PFI Forum
forum.paganfederation.org

The Pagan Library
www.paganlibrary.com

Pagan Moon
www.paganmoononline.com

Pagan Music Discussion
www.paganmusic.com/discussion.htm

Pagan Network Forums
www.pagan-network.org/forums

Pagan Stuff Cheap
www.paganstuffcheap.com

Pagan Traditions & Discussion
www.paganforum.com

Raven and Crone
www.ravenandcrone.com

RealPagan - Paganism for the Real World
www.realpagan.net/forum

Reformed Druids of North America
www.rdna.info

Religion Facts
www.religionfacts.com

Sacred Mists Shoppe
www.sacredmists.com

The Blessed Bee
www.theblessedbee.com

The Magickal Cat
www.theMagickalcat.com

The Mystic Cauldron
www.mysticcauldron.com

The Mystic Corner

www.themysticcorner.com

The Official Witch Shoppe
www.theofficialwitchshoppe.net

The Old Age Metaphysical Country Store
www.metaphysical-store.com

The Round Table
www.rationalpagans.com

The White Goddess - Pagan Portal
www.thewhitegoddess.co.uk

White Magick Alchemy
www.whiteMagickalchemy.com

Wiccan Cauldron
www.wiccancauldron.com

The Wiccan Way
www.wiccanway.com

WikiPagan
pagan.wikia.com

Witch Forum
www.witchforum.net

Index

Feeding Baby
Cynthia Cherry
978-1941070000

Axolotl
Lolly Brown
978-0989658430

Dysautonomia, POTS
Syndrome
Frederick Earlstein
978-0989658485

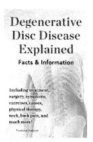

Degenerative Disc
Disease Explained
Frederick Earlstein
978-0989658485

Sinusitis, Hay Fever,
Allergic Rhinitis Explained
Frederick Earlstein
978-1941070024

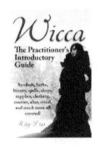

Wicca
Riley Star
978-1941070130

Zombie Apocalypse
Rex Cutty
978-1941070154

Capybara
Lolly Brown
978-1941070062

Eels As Pets
Lolly Brown
978-1941070167

Scabies and Lice Explained
Frederick Earlstein
978-1941070017

Saltwater Fish As Pets
Lolly Brown
978-0989658461

Torticollis Explained
Frederick Earlstein
978-1941070055

Kennel Cough
Lolly Brown
978-0989658409

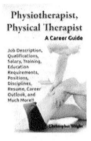

Physiotherapist, Physical
Therapist
Christopher Wright
978-0989658492

Rats, Mice, and Dormice
As Pets
Lolly Brown
978-1941070079

Wallaby and Wallaroo Care
Lolly Brown
978-1941070031

Bodybuilding Supplements
Explained
Jon Shelton
978-1941070239

Demonology
Riley Star
978-19401070314

Pigeon Racing
Lolly Brown
978-1941070307

Dwarf Hamster
Lolly Brown
978-1941070390

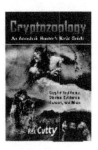

Cryptozoology
Rex Cutty
978-1941070406

Eye Strain
Frederick Earlstein
978-1941070369

Inez The Miniature Elephant
Asher Ray
978-1941070353

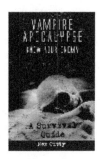

Vampire Apocalypse
Rex Cutty
978-1941070321

Made in United States
Orlando, FL
24 June 2024